P9-DWI-246

The Origin of Others

The Charles Eliot Norton Lectures, 2016

TONI MORRISON

The Origin of Others

With a Foreword by Ta-Nehisi Coates

HARVARD UNIVERSITY PRESS

Cambridge, Massachusetts
London, England

2017

Copyright © 2017 by Toni Morrison

Foreword © 2017 by Ta-Nehisi Coates

All rights reserved

Printed in the United States of America

FOURTH PRINTING

*Cataloging-in-Publication Data available from the
Library of Congress*

ISBN: 978-0-674-97645-0

Contents

Foreword by Ta-Nehisi Coates

In the spring of 2016 Toni Morrison delivered a series of talks at Harvard University on "the literature of belonging." It is no surprise, given the nature of Morrison's remarkable catalogue, that she turned her eye to the subject of race. Morrison's lectures came at an auspicious time. Barack Obama was then entering the last year of his two-term presidency. His approval ratings were rising. The insurgent Black Lives Matter movement had pushed police brutality to the front of the national conversation, and unlike most "conversations on race," this one netted results. Obama's two black attorneys general, Eric Holder and Loretta Lynch, had launched investigations into police departments across the country. Reports emerged out of Ferguson, Chicago, and Baltimore substantiating the kind of systemic racism that had long been confined mainly to anecdote. This aggressive approach was expected to continue under the country's first woman president, Hillary Clinton, who was, at the time Morrison began her series, heavily favored against a man the world considered a political lightweight. All of this testified to a country intent on defying the precepts of history and at last approaching the justice end of the moral universe's long arc.

And then the arc got longer.

The first reaction to Donald Trump's victory was to minimize what it said about American racism. A cottage industry sprang up asserting that the 2016 election was a populist uprising against Wall Street fomented by those left out of the new economy. Clinton was said to have been doomed by a focus on "identity politics." These arguments often carried the seeds of their own undoing. No one ever explained how it was that those most often left behind by this new economy—black and brown workers— never found their way into the Trump coalition. Moreover, some of the very critics of Clinton's "identity politics" had no problem deploying those politics themselves. Senator Bernie Sanders, Clinton's primary opponent, could be heard one week extolling his roots in the white working class, and then the next urging Democrats to get "beyond" identity politics. All identity politics are not created equal, it seems.

The Origin of Others—Morrison's new book derived from the lecture series she gave at Harvard—is not directly concerned with the rise of Donald Trump. But it is impossible to read her thoughts on belonging, on who fits under the umbrella of society and who does not, without considering our current moment. *Origin* conducts its inquiry on the field of American history and thus addresses itself to the oldest and most potent form of identity politics in American history—the identity politics of racism. This is a work about the creation of aliens and the erection of fences, one that employs literary criticism, history, and memoir in an attempt to understand how and why we have come to associate those fences with pigment.

Morrison's book joins a body of work, evolving over the last century, that has effectively argued for the indelible nature of white racism. Her confederates include Sven Beckert and Edward Baptist, who've revealed the violent nature of that racism and the profits reaped from it; James McPherson and Eric Foner, who've shown how that racism birthed the Civil War and then undermined the country's effort to reconstruct itself; Beryl Satter and Ira Katznelson, who've explained how racism corrupted the New Deal; and Kahlil Gibran Muhammad and Bruce Western, who've shown how, in our time, that racism paved the way for the era of mass incarceration.

But the closest cousin to Morrison's work is probably *Racecraft,* the book by Barbara Fields and Karen Fields that argues Americans have sought to erase the crime of racism, which is active, with the concept of race, which is not. When we say "race" as opposed to "racism," we reify the idea that race is somehow a feature of the natural world and racism the predictable result of it. Despite the body of scholarship that has accumulated to show that this formulation is backwards, that racism precedes race, Americans still haven't quite gotten the point. And so we find ourselves speaking of "racial segregation," "the racial chasm," "the racial divide," "racial profiling," or "racial diversity"— as though each of these ideas is grounded in something beyond our own making. The impact of this is not insignificant. If "race" is the work of genes or the gods, or both, then we can forgive ourselves for never having unworked the problem.

Morrison's inquiry proceeds from the less comfortable space which holds that race is only tangentially about genes. From there she aids our understanding of how a concept that seems so flimsy could have such a strong hold over millions of people. The need to confirm one's humanity while committing inhumane acts is key, Morrison argues. She looks at the accounts of the planter Thomas Thistlewood, who records his serial rape of enslaved women in his diary with all the ease of reporting the shearing of sheep. "Sliced in between his sexual activities are his notes on farming, chores, visitors, illness, etc.," Morrison tells us chillingly. What manner of psychological work did Thistlewood have to do to become so callous to rape? The psychological work of Othering—of convincing oneself that there is some sort of natural and divine delineation between the enslaver and the enslaved. After analyzing the vicious beatings that an enslaved Mary Prince receives from her mistress, Morrison says:

> The necessity of rendering the slave a foreign species appears to be a desperate attempt to confirm one's own self as normal. The urgency of distinguishing between those who belong to the human race and those who are decidedly non-human is so powerful the spotlight turns away and shines not on the object of degradation but on its creator. Even assuming exaggeration by the slaves, the sensibility of slave owners is gothic. It's as though they are shouting, "I am not a beast! I'm not a beast! I torture the helpless to prove I am not weak." The danger of sympathizing with the stranger is the possibility of becoming a stranger. To lose one's racial-ized rank is to lose one's own valued and enshrined difference.

Morrison is speaking of enslavers and the en-slaved, but her point about rank holds true today. The past few years have seen a steady parade of videos in which American police officers are shown beating, tasing, choking, and shooting black people for relatively mild infractions or no infraction at all. African-Americans, as well as many other Americans, have been horrified. And yet the language of justification has proven familiar. When Officer Darren Wilson killed Michael Brown he reported that Brown appeared to be "bulking up to run through the shots," an act that rendered Brown as something more, but ultimately something less, than human. The sub-human aspect to the killing was reinforced by the decision to leave Brown's body to bake on the concrete in the middle of summer. Rendering Brown as a kind of monster justifies his murder and allows a force of officers who—according to the Justice Department report—were little more than gangsters to consider themselves legitimate, to consider themselves perfectly human.

Racist dehumanization is not merely symbolic—it delineates the borders of power. "Race," writes the historian Nell Painter, "is an idea, not a fact." In America, part of the idea of race is that whiteness automatically confers a decreased chance of dying like Michael Brown, or Walter Scott, or Eric Garner. And death is but the superlative example of what it means to live as an "Other," to exist beyond the border of a great "belonging." The kind of "economic anxiety" that allegedly drove voters into the arms of Donald Trump would represent a significant step up for most black people. In the Republican primary, the median household income for a Trump voter was roughly double the median income for the average black family in America. The current wave of sympathy confronting a mostly (though not entirely) white opioid epidemic is of a different piece from the wave of condemnation that was brought to bear during the crack crisis of the 1980s. The current wave of concern greeting the increased mortality rates among certain white men is of a different piece from the resigned apathy which accompanies the high mortality rates that have always haunted black life in this country.

Racism matters. To be an Other in this country matters—and the disheartening truth is that it will likely continue to matter. Human communities rarely cede privileges out of simple altruism, and thus the only world in which one can imagine the subscribers of whiteness renouncing their religion is a world in which its privileges become a luxury they can ill afford. We have seen moments like this in American history. A prolonged civil war led whites to conclude that blacks were fit to die in their ranks. A cold war with the Soviet Union turned the Jim Crow South into a global embarrassment and a propaganda boon for the country's enemies. And the governance of George W. Bush, the quagmire of war on two fronts, an economy in free fall, and the federal government's massive failure in the wake of Hurricane

Katrina paved the way for its first black president. A wave of hope greeted each of these cases, a sense that the country had somehow defeated history. And in each of these cases that hope was ultimately frustrated.

To understand why we find ourselves here again, we are fortunate to have Toni Morrison, one of the finest writers and thinkers this country has ever produced. Her work is rooted in history and pulls beauty from some of its most grotesque manifestations. But that beauty is not fantasy, and so it should not be surprising that she ranks among those who understand the hold that history has on us all. *The Origin of Others* expounds on that understanding, and if it does not demonstrate an immediate escape from the grip of the past, it is a welcome aid in grappling with how that grip came to be.

The Origin of Others

I

Romancing Slavery

WE STILL played on the floor, my sister and I, so it must have been 1932 or 1933 when we heard she was coming. Millicent MacTeer, our great-grandmother. An often quoted legend, she was scheduled to visit all of the relatives' houses in the neighborhood. She lived in Michigan, a much-sought-after midwife. Her visit to Ohio had been long anticipated because she was regarded as the wise, unquestionable, majestic head of our family. The majesty was clear when something I had never witnessed before happened as she entered a room: without urging, all the males stood up.

Finally, after a round of visits with other relatives, she entered our living room, tall, straight-backed, leaning on a cane she obviously did not need, and greeted my mother. Then, staring at my sister and me, playing or simply sitting on the floor, she frowned, pointed her cane at us, and said, "These children have been tampered with." My mother objected (strenuously), but the damage was done. My great-grandmother was tar black, and my mother knew precisely what she meant: we, her children, and therefore our immediate family, were sullied, not pure.

Learning so early (or being taught when one doesn't know better) the ingredients of being lesser because Other didn't impress me then, probably because I was preternaturally arrogant and overwhelmed with devotion to myself. "Tampered with" sounded exotic at first—like something desirable. When my mother defied her own grandmother, it became clear that "tampered with" meant lesser, if not completely Other.

Descriptions of cultural, racial, and physical differences that note "Otherness" but remain free of categories of worth or rank are difficult to come by. Many, if not most, textual / literary descriptions of race range from the sly, the nuanced, to the pseudo-scientifically "proven." And all have justifications and claims of accuracy in order to sustain dominance. We are aware of strategies for survival in the natural world: distraction / sacrifice to protect the nest; pack hunting / chasing food on the hoof. But for humans as an advanced species, our tendency to separate and judge those not in our clan as the enemy, as the vulnerable and the deficient needing control, has a long history not limited to the animal world or prehistoric man. Race has been a constant arbiter of difference, as have wealth, class, and gender—each of which is about power and the necessity of control.

One has only to read the eugenics of the Southern physician and slaveholder Samuel Cartwright to understand the lengths to which science, if not politics, can go in documenting the need for control of the Other.

"According to unalterable physiological laws," he writes in his "Report on the Diseases and Physical Peculiarities of the Negro Race" (1851), "negroes, as a general rule, to which there are but few exceptions, can only have their intellectual faculties awakened in a sufficient degree to receive moral culture, and to profit by religious or other instruction, when under the compulsatory authority of the white man. . . . From their natural indolence, unless under the stimulus of compulsion, they doze away their lives with the capacity of their lungs for atmospheric air only half expanded, from the want of exercise. . . . The black blood distributed to the brain chains the mind to ignorance, superstition and barbarism, and bolts the door against civilization, moral culture and religious truth." Dr. Cartwright pointed to two illnesses, one of which he labeled "drapetomania, or the disease causing slaves to run away." The other illness he diagnosed as "dysaesthesia aethiopica"—a kind of mental lethargy that caused the negro "to be like a person half asleep" (what slaveholders more commonly identified as "rascality"). One wonders why, if these slaves were such a burden and threat, they were so eagerly bought, sold. We learn at last their benefit: the forced "exercise, so beneficial to the negro, is expended in cultivating . . . cotton, sugar, rice and tobacco, which, but for his labor . . . go uncultivated, and their products lost to the world. Both parties are benefitted—the negro as well as his master."

These observations were not casual opinions. They were printed in the *New Orleans Medical and Surgical Journal.* The point being that blacks are useful, not quite like cattle, yet not recognizably human.

Similar diatribes have been employed by virtually every group on earth—with or without power—to enforce their beliefs by constructing an Other.

One purpose of scientific racism is to identify an outsider in order to define one's self. Another possibility is to maintain (even enjoy) one's own difference without contempt for the categorized difference of the Othered. Literature is especially and obviously revelatory in exposing/contemplating the definition of self whether it condemns or supports the means by which it is acquired.

How does one become a racist, a sexist? Since no one is born a racist and there is no fetal predisposition to sexism, one learns Othering not by lecture or instruction but by example.

It was probably universally clear—to sellers as well as the sold—that slavery was an inhuman, though profitable, condition. The sellers certainly didn't want to be enslaved; the purchased often committed suicide to avoid it. So how did it work? One of the ways nations could accommodate slavery's degradation was by brute force; another was to romance it.

In 1750, a young upper-class Englishman—a second son who probably could not inherit under the laws of primogeniture—set out to make his fortune first as an overseer and then as an owner of slaves and his own sugar plantation in Jamaica. His name was Thomas Thistlewood, and his life, exploits, and thoughts are carefully researched and recorded by Douglas Hall as one of a series of scholarly texts, in Macmillan's Warwick University Caribbean Studies Series, later reprinted by the University of the West Indies Press. This particular volume contains excerpts of Thistlewood's papers along with Douglas Hall's comments and was published in 1987 as *In Miserable Slavery*. Like Samuel Pepys, Thistlewood kept a minutely detailed diary—a diary minus reflection or sustained judgment, just the facts. Events, encounters with other people, weather, negotiations, prices, losses, all of which either interested him or he felt required notation. He had no plans to publish or share the information he recorded. A reading of his diaries reveals that, like most of his countrymen, he had a seamless commitment to the status quo. He did not wonder about slavery's morality or his place in its scheme. He merely existed in the world as he found it and recorded it. It is this, his divorce from moral judgment, not at all atypical, that sheds light on slavery's acceptance. Among the intimate marks of his exhaustive note-taking are details of his sexual life on the plantation (not different from his youthful and primarily casual British exploits).

He noted the time of the encounter, its level of satisfaction, the frequency of the act, and, especially, where it took place. Other than the obvious pleasure were the ease and comfort of control. There was no need for seduction or even conversation—just a mere notation among others about the price of sugarcane or a successful negotiation for flour. Unlike Thistlewood's business notations, his carnal record was written in Latin: *Sup. Lect.* for "on the bed"; *Sup. Terr.* for "on the ground"; *In Silva* for "in the woods"; *In Mag.* or *Parv. Dom.* for "in

the great" or "small room"; and, when not sat-
isfied, *Sed non bene.* These days, I suppose, we
would call it rape; those days it was called *droit
du seigneur,* right of the lord. Sliced in between
his sexual activities are his notes on farming,
chores, visitors, illnesses, etc.

An entry from September 10, 1751, reads in
part: "about 1/2 past 10 A.M. *Cum* Flora, a congo,
Super Terram among the canes, above the wall
head, right hand of the river, toward the Negro
ground. She had been for water cress. Gave her
4 bitts." The next day, in the early hours of the
morning, he writes: "About 2 A.M. *Cum* Negroe
girl, *super* floor, at north bed foot, in the east
parlor, 'unknown.'" And an entry from June 2,
1760, reads in part: "Cleaned about the works,
threw up the wood hoops, carrying out pond
earth, &c. P.M. *Cum* L. Mimber, *Sup Me Lect.*"

Different, but no less revelatory, are the literary attempts to "romance" slavery, to render it
acceptable, even preferable, by humanizing, even
cherishing, it. Control, benign or rapacious,

may ultimately not be necessary. See? Says Harriet Beecher Stowe to her (white) readers. Calm down, she says. Slaves control themselves. Don't be afraid. Negroes only want to serve. The slave's natural instinct, she implies, is toward kindness—an instinct that is disrupted only by vicious whites who, like Simon Legree (significantly, a Northerner by birth), threaten and abuse them. The sense of fear and disdain that white people may have, one that encourages brutality, is, she implies, unwarranted. Almost. Almost. Yet there are in *Uncle Tom's Cabin* signs of Stowe's own fear, literary protection, as it were. Or perhaps she is simply sensitive to the reader's apprehension. How, for example, do you make it safe in the nineteenth century to enter Black Space? Do you simply knock and enter? If unarmed, do you enter at all? Well, even if you are an innocent young boy, such as Master George, going to visit Uncle Tom and Aunt Chloe, you need excessive, benign signs of welcome, of safety. Tom's house is a humble shack, small and right next to the master's home. Yet for Stowe the white boy's entrance needs obvious signs of safe passage. Therefore Stowe describes the entrance as outrageously inviting:

> In front [the cabin] had a neat garden-patch, where, every summer, strawberries, raspberries, and a variety of fruits and vegetables, flourished under careful tending. The whole front . . . was covered by a large scarlet bignonia and a native multiflora rose, which, entwisting and interlacing, left scarce a vestige of the rough logs to be seen. Here, also, in summer, various brilliant annuals, such as marigolds, petunias, four-o'clocks, found an indulgent corner in which to unfold their splendors. . . .

The natural beauty Stowe is at pains to describe is cultivated, welcoming, seductive, and excessive.

Once inside this tiny log cabin where Aunt Chloe is cooking and managing everyone, following some gossip and compliments, they all sit down to eat. Except the children, Mose and Pete. They are fed under the table, on the floor. With chunks of food thrown toward them, and for which they scramble:

[Master] George and Tom moved to a comfortable seat in the chimney-corner, while Aunt Chloe, after baking a goodly pile of cakes, took her baby on her lap, and began alternately filling its mouth and her own, and distributing to Mose and Pete, who seemed rather to prefer eating theirs as they rolled about on the floor under the table, tickling each other, and occasionally pulling the baby's toes.

"O! go long, will ye?" said the mother, giving now and then a kick, in a kind of general way, under the table, when the movement became too obstreperous. "Can't ye be decent when white folks comes to see ye? Stop dat ar, now, will ye? Better mind yerselves, or I'll take ye down a button-hole lower, when Mas'r George is gone!"

That, to me, is an extraordinary scene: the young master has declared himself full, and you—a slave mother—hold your infant in your arms and feed him and yourself while your "husband" eats also, but you throw food on a dirt floor for your two other children to scramble for? An odd scene designed to amuse, I think, and reassure the reader that everything in this atmosphere is safe, even amusing and especially kind, generous, and subservient. These are carefully demarcated passages intended to quiet the fearful white reader.

Harriet Beecher Stowe did not write *Uncle Tom's Cabin* for Tom, Aunt Chloe, or any black people to read. Her contemporary readership was white people, those who needed, wanted, or could relish the romance.

For Thistlewood, rape is the ownership romance of *droit du seigneur.* For Stowe, slavery is sexually and romantically sanitized and perfumed. The relationship of little Eva and Topsy—in which Topsy, an unruly, simpleminded black child, is redeemed, civilized by a loving white child—is so profoundly sentimentalized that it becomes another prime example of the romance of slavery.

In a profound way, I owe a debt to my greatgrandmother. Although she had no intentions of being helpful—she had no remedy for our deficiency—she nevertheless awakened in me an inquiry that has influenced much of my writing. *The Bluest Eye* was my initial exploration of the harm of racial self-loathing. Later I examined the concept of its opposite, racial superiority, in *Paradise.* Again in *God Help the Child* I looked at the triumphalism and deception that colorism fosters. I wrote about its flaws, arrogance, and ultimately its self-destruction. Now (in my current novel-in-progress) I am excited to explore the education of a racist—how does one move from a non-racial womb to the womb of racism, to belonging to a specific loved or despised yet race-inflected existence? What is race (other than genetic imagination) and why does it matter? Once its parameters are known, defined (if at all possible), what behavior does it demand / encourage? Race is the classification of a species, and we are the human race, period. Then what is this other thing—the hostility, the social racism, the Othering?

What is the nature of Othering's comfort, its allure, its power (social, psychological, or economical)? Is it the thrill of belonging—which implies being part of something bigger than one's solo self, and therefore stronger? My initial view leans toward the social / psychological need for a "stranger," an Other in order to define the estranged self (the crowd seeker is always the lonely one).

Lastly, let me quote from *The Romance of Race,* Jolie A. Sheffer's excellent rendition of the means by which "belonging," that is, creating a coherent nation out of immigrants, took place during the great immigration from southern and eastern Europe:

> [S]ome 23 million immigrants, mostly from eastern and southern Europe, and overwhelmingly Jewish, Catholic, and Orthodox, arrived in the United States in the period between 1890 and 1920, challenging the white Anglo-Saxon Protestant (WASP) majority. Such "infusions of alien blood," in turn-of-the-twentieth-century parlance, transformed U.S. national identity, but . . . did not fundamentally challenge white hegemony; rather, European ethnics soon became, at least nominally, part of the "white" majority.

The scholarship on this subject is deep and wide. These immigrants to the United States understood that if they wanted to become "real" Americans they must sever or at least greatly downplay their ties to their native country, in order to embrace their whiteness. The definition of "Americanness" (sadly) remains color for many people.

2

Being or Becoming the Stranger

Because there are such major benefits in creating and sustaining an Other, it is important to 1) identify the benefits and 2) discover what may be the social / political results of repudiating those benefits.

Flannery O'Connor exhibits with honesty and profound perception her understanding of the stranger, the outcast, the Other. Underneath the comedy, often noted by her reviewers, lies a quick and accurate reading of the construction of the stranger and its benefits. Representative of this deliberate education in escaping rather than becoming the stranger, the perennial Other, is her short story "The Artificial Nigger." The story is a carefully rendered description of how and why blacks are so vital to a white definition of humanity. In that process, as we shall see, the word "nigger" is used constantly, even when and especially when it is unnecessary. Its use is a large part of the education of the young white boy in the story. The insistent and excessive use indicates how important blacks are to the self-regard of his uncle, Mr. Head.

O'Connor opens her story with a feint, a deliberately misleading description: Mr. Head is introduced to the reader in language invoking aristocratic symbols of royalty.

Mr. Head awakened to discover that the room was full of moonlight. He sat up and stared at the floor boards—the color of silver—and then at the ticking on his pillow, which might have been brocade,

and after a second, he saw half of the moon
five feet away in his shaving mirror, paused
as if it were waiting for his permission to
enter. It rolled forward and cast a digni-
fying light on everything. The straight
chair against the wall looked stiff and at-
tentive as if it were awaiting an order and
Mr. Head's trousers, hanging to the back
of it, had an almost noble air, like the gar-
ment some great man had just flung to his
servant. . . .

There are some one hundred fifty words before
the reader learns, contrary to Mr. Head's
dreams, of his rural poverty, his age, and his
sadness. Learns also of his current purpose in
life—to educate his nephew, Nelson, in the
process of Othering, of identifying the stranger.
When, on a train to Atlanta, they see an obviously prosperous black man pass by, the racist
instruction sharpens.

"What was that?"[Mr. Head] asked.

"A man," the boy said, and gave him an indignant look as if he were tired of having his intelligence insulted.

"What kind of a man?" Mr. Head persisted, his voice expressionless.

"A fat man," Nelson said. . . .

"You don't know what kind?" Mr. Head said in a final tone.

"An old man," the boy said. . . .

"That was a nigger," Mr. Head said and sat back. . . .

"You said they were black. . . . You never said they were tan. . . ."

This process of identifying the stranger has an expected response—exaggerated fear of the stranger.

Later, when lost in the streets of the city and finding themselves in a black neighborhood, they are of course alarmed: "Black eyes in black faces were watching them from every direction."

When in desperation they stop before a black woman standing barefoot on her porch, Nelson has a strange sensation: "He suddenly wanted her to reach down and pick him up and draw him against her and then he wanted to feel her breath on his face . . . while she held him tighter and tighter. He had never had such a feeling before." The woman kindly, nonchalantly, gives them directions. Soon there is the consequence of this non-threatening encounter: disagreement, abandonment, treachery, between Mr. Head and Nelson. Without the glue of racial superiority there seems to be no possibility of forgiveness or re-union. When finally they enter an all-white neighborhood, their fear of not belonging, of becoming, themselves, the stranger, destabilizes them. They are calmed and rescued from this threat only by seeing a visual connection to what they believe is a shared racism of whites of all classes—the artificial nigger. Standing before the figure, the statue of a black jockey, they gaze at it "as if they were faced with some great mystery, some monument to another's victory that brought them together in their common defeat. They could both feel it dissolving their differences like an action of mercy."

The education of the boy is complete: He has been successfully and artfully taught racism and believes he has acquired respectability, status. And the illusion of power through the process of inventing an Other.

This twentieth-century perception of the stranger must be placed alongside earlier narratives written or recorded by the stranger in which he details his own perception of himself. First it might be valuable to research "race" itself. Racial identification and exclusion did not begin, or end, with blacks. Culture, physical traits, religion were and are among all precursors of strategies for ascendance and power. One has only to recall the history of the term "Caucasian," its uses and its decline.

An exhaustive explanation is given in Bruce Baum's book *The Rise and Fall of the Caucasian*

Race. "Since 1952," he writes, "the 'Caucasian Race' category has retained a prominent place in everyday discourse about race, particularly in the United States, but it has increasingly been called into question by anthropologists and biologists, along with the 'race' concept itself." "Leaving aside the views of certain white supremacists," he continues, "it now generally goes without saying that there is no such thing as the Aryan race. The 'Aryan race' myth was cobbled together from various sources in the mid-nineteenth century . . . before it became a lynch pin for Nazism. . . . By contrast, the notion of a Caucasian race has gone in and out of vogue, and then back into vogue, among raciologists and in popular usage." Baum concludes, among other things, "Race, in short, is an effect of power."

So when we speak or write of the stranger, the outsider, the Other, we should keep in mind what the relationship signifies.

The narratives of slaves, both written and spoken, are critical to understanding the process of Othering. Several of their narratives begin in childhood with descriptions of love for and devotion to their original owners and deep sorrow at being sold away. The innocence of children—owned and owners alike—is a staple of slave narratives: idealized in theater, commercial and artistic books, posters, and newspapers. It is only later, as they approach puberty, that an alternate universe is revealed. But it is a universe in which being literally enslaved, being the despised and abused Other, shines its most revealing light on the enslavers—those who relished, maintained, and profited from the so-called peculiar institution.

I'd like to call your attention to examples of the human cost of free slave labor that earned profit for the owners. These examples I have drawn from Mary Prince's memoir *The History of Mary Prince, A West Indian Slave* (1831).

Consider this excerpt from Prince's recollections of working in the salt mines: "I was given a half barrel [to be filled with salt] and a shovel, and had to stand up to my knees in the water, from four o'clock in the morning till nine, when we were given some Indian corn boiled in water. . . . We . . . worked through the heat of the day . . . the sun . . . raising salt blisters. . . . Our feet and legs, from standing in the water for so many hours, soon became full of dreadful boils, which eat down in some cases to the very bone. . . . We slept in a long shed, divided into narrow slips, like the stalls used for cattle." She describes leaving one master for another as "going from one butcher to another. . . . [The first one] used to beat me while raging and foaming with passion . . . [the next one] was usually quite calm. He would stand by and give orders for a slave to be cruelly whipped . . . walking about and taking snuff with the greatest composure."

If these descriptions are not explicit examples of sadism, it's hard to think what is.

Or consider this account, also from Mary Prince's memoir: "One day a heavy squall of wind and rain came on suddenly, and my mistress sent me round the corner of the house to empty a large earthen jar. The jar was already cracked with an old deep crack that divided it in the middle, and in turning it upside down to empty it, it parted in my hand. . . . I ran crying to my mistress, 'O mistress, the jar has come in two.' 'You have broken it, have you?' she replied. . . . She stripped and flogged me long and severely with the cow-skin; as long as she had strength to use the lash, for she did not give over till she was quite tired."

Nothing will undo the accident; nothing will immediately repair the jar, so what is the urgency of the beating? To teach a lesson or to enjoy it? Mary Prince knew how the treatment of slaves degraded the owner, as did Harriet Jacobs, whose *Incidents in the Life of a Slave Girl* (1861) appeared thirty long years after Prince's memoir, on the eve of the Civil War. Jacobs writes: "I can testify, from my own experience and observation, that slavery is a curse to the whites as well as to the blacks. It makes the white fathers cruel and sensual; the sons violent and licentious; it contaminates the daughters, and makes the wives wretched."

As fascinatingly repulsive as these incidents of violence are, to my mind the question that surfaces, one that is far more revealing than the severity of the punishment, is, who are these people? How hard they work to define the slave as inhuman, savage, when in fact the definition of the inhuman describes overwhelmingly the punisher. When they rest, exhausted, between bouts of lashing, the punishment is more sadistic than corrective. If sustained whipping tires the lasher, and he or she must take a series of breaks before continuing, what good does its duration do to the whipped? Such extreme pain seems to be designed for the pleasure of the one with the lash.

The necessity of rendering the slave a foreign species appears to be a desperate attempt to confirm one's own self as normal. The urgency of distinguishing between those who belong to the human race and those who are decidedly non-human is so powerful the spotlight turns away and shines not on the object of degradation but on its creator. Even assuming exaggeration by the slaves, the sensibility of slave owners is gothic. It's as though they are shouting, "I am not a beast! I'm not a beast! I torture the helpless to prove I am not weak." The danger of sympathizing with the stranger is the possibility of becoming a stranger. To lose one's racial-ized rank is to lose one's own valued and enshrined difference.

I have rendered and explored this conundrum in almost every book I have written. In *A Mercy* I labored to identify the journey from sympathetic race relations to violent ones fostered by religion. An erstwhile kind mistress becomes punitive to her slaves after she is widowed and joins a strict and severe religious sect. There she gains prestige, lost because of widowhood, by abusing her slaves.

My most theatrical exploration is apparent in *Paradise.* There I examined the contradictory results of devising a purely raced community—only this time the "stranger" is every white or "mixed-race" person.

Perhaps I can clarify this prevalent capacity to estrange others by explaining how I myself participated in the process and learned from it. I have published this account elsewhere, but I want to describe to you how vulnerable we are to distancing ourselves and forcing our own images onto strangers as well as becoming the stranger we may abhor.

I am in this river place—newly mine—walking in the yard when I see a woman sitting on the seawall at the edge of a neighbor's garden. A homemade fishing pole arcs into the water some twenty feet from her hand. A feeling of welcome washes over me. I walk toward her, right up to the fence that separates my place from the neighbor's, and notice with pleasure the clothes she wears: men's shoes, a man's hat, a well-worn colorless sweater over a long black dress. She is black. The woman turns her head and greets me with an easy smile and a "How you doing?" She tells me her name (Mother Something) and we talk for some time—fifteen minutes or so—about fish recipes and weather and children. When I ask her if she lives there she answers, no. She lives in a nearby village, but the owner of the house lets her come to this spot any time she wants to fish, and she comes every week, sometimes several days in a row when the perch or catfish are running and even if they aren't because she likes eel, too, and they were always there. She is witty and full of the wisdom that older women always seem to have a lock on. When we part, it is with an understanding that she will be there the next day or very soon after and we will visit again. I imagine more conversations with her. I will invite her into my house for coffee, for tales, for laughter. She reminds me of someone, something. I imagine a friendship, casual, effortless, delightful.

She is not there the next day. She is not there the following days either. And I look for her every morning. The summer passes and I have not seen her at all. Finally I approach the neighbor to ask about her and am bewildered to learn that the neighbor does not know who or what I am talking about. No old woman fished from her wall—ever—and none had permission to do so. I decide that the fisherwoman fibbed about the permission and took advantage of the neighbor's frequent absences to poach. The fact of the neighbor's presence is proof that the fisherwoman would not be there. During the months following, I ask lots of people if they know Mother Something. No one, not even people who have lived in nearby villages for seventy years, has ever heard of her.

I felt cheated, puzzled, but also amused, and I wonder off and on if I have dreamed her. In any case, I tell myself, it was an encounter of no value other than anecdotal. Still. Little by little, annoyance then bitterness takes the place of my original bewilderment. A certain view from my windows is now devoid of her, reminding me every morning of her deceit and my disappointment. What was she doing in that neighborhood anyway? She didn't drive, had to walk four miles if indeed she lived where she said she did. How could she be missed on the road in that hat, those awful shoes? I try to understand the intensity of my chagrin, and why I am missing a woman I spoke to for fifteen minutes. I get nowhere except for the stingy explanation that she had come into my space (next to it anyway—at the property line, at the edge, just at the fence where the most interesting things always happen), and had implied promises of female comradery, of opportunities for me to be generous, of protection and protecting. Now she is gone, taking with her my good opinion of myself, which, of course, is unforgivable. And isn't that the kind of thing that we fear strangers will do? Disturb. Betray. Prove they are not like us? That is why it is so hard to know what to do with them. The love that prophets have urged us to offer the stranger is the same love which Jean-Paul Sartre could reveal as the very mendacity of Hell. The signal line of *No Exit,* "L'enfer c'est les autres," raises the possibility that "other people" are responsible for turning a personal world into a public hell. Hell is other people.

In the admonition of a prophet and the sly warning of an artist, strangers as well as the beloved are understood to tempt our gaze to slide away or to stake claims. Religious prophets caution against the slide, the looking away; Sartre warns against love as possession.

The resources available to us for benign access to each other, for vaulting the mere blue air that separates us, are few but powerful: language, image, and experience, which may involve both, one, or neither of the first two. Language (saying, listening, reading) can encourage, even mandate, surrender, the breach of distances among us, whether they are continental or on the same pillow, whether they are distances of culture or the distinctions and indistinctions of age or gender, whether they are the consequences of social invention or biology. Image increasingly rules the realm of shaping, sometimes becoming, often contaminating, knowledge. Provoking language or eclipsing it, an image can determine not only what we know and feel but also what we believe is worth knowing about what we feel.

These two godlings, language and image, feed and form experience. My instant embrace of an outrageously dressed fisherwoman was due in part to an image on which my representation of her was based. I immediately sentimentalized and appropriated her. Fantasized her as my personal shaman. I owned her or wanted to (and I suspect she glimpsed it). I had forgotten the power of embedded images and stylish language to seduce, reveal, control. Forgot too their capacity to help us pursue the human project—which is to remain human and to block the dehumanization and estrangement of others.

But something unforeseen has entered into this admittedly oversimplified menu of our resources. Far from our original expectations of increased intimacy and broader knowledge, routine media presentations deploy images and language that narrow our view of what humans look like (or ought to look like) and what in fact we are like. Succumbing to the perversions of media can blur vision; resisting them can do the same. I was clearly and aggressively resisting such influences in my encounter with the fisherwoman. Art and the imagination as well as the market can be complicit in the sequestering of form from formula, of nature from artifice, of humanity from commodity. Art gesturing toward representation has, in some exalted quarters, become literally beneath contempt. The concept of what it is to be human has altered, and the word "truth" so needs quotation marks around it that its absence (its elusiveness) is stronger than its presence.

Why should we want to know a stranger when it is easier to estrange another? Why should we want to close the distance when we can close the gate? Appeals in art and religion for comity in the Common Wealth are faint.

It took some time for me to understand my unreasonable claims on that fisherwoman. To understand that I was longing for and missing some aspect of myself, and that there are no strangers. There are only versions of ourselves, many of which we have not embraced, most of which we wish to protect ourselves from. For the stranger is not foreign, she is random; not alien but remembered; and it is the randomness of the encounter with our already known— although unacknowledged—selves that summons a ripple of alarm. That makes us reject the figure and the emotions it provokes—especially when these emotions are profound. It is also what makes us want to own, govern, and administrate the Other. To romance her, if we can, back into our own mirrors. In either instance (of alarm or false reverence), we deny her personhood, the specific individuality we insist upon for ourselves.

3

The Color Fetish

Of constant fascination for me are the ways in which literature employs skin color to reveal character or drive narrative—especially if the fictional main character is white (which is almost always the case). Whether it is the horror of one drop of the mystical "black" blood, or signs of innate white superiority, or of deranged and excessive sexual power, the framing and the meaning of color are often the deciding factor.

For the horror that the "one-drop" rule excites, there is no better guide than William Faulkner. What else haunts *The Sound and the Fury* or *Absalom, Absalom!*? Between the marital outrages incest and miscegenation, the latter (an old but useful term for "the mixing of races") is obviously the more abhorrent. In much American literature, when plot requires a family crisis, nothing is more disgusting than mutual sexual congress between the races. It is the mutual aspect of these encounters that is rendered shocking, illegal, and repulsive. Unlike the rape of slaves, human choice or, God forbid, love receives wholesale condemnation. And for Faulkner they lead to murder.

In Chapter IV of *Absalom, Absalom!* Mr. Compson explains to Quentin what drove Henry Sutpen to kill his half-brother Charles Bon:

And yet, four years later, Henry had to kill Bon to keep them from marrying. . . .

Yes, granted that, even to the unworldly Henry, let alone the more traveled father, the existence of the eighth part negro mistress and the sixteenth part negro son, granted even the morganatic ceremony . . . was reason enough. . . .

Much later in the novel Quentin imagines this exchange between Henry and Charles:

—So it's the miscegenation, not the incest which you can't bear. . . .

Henry doesn't answer.

—And he sent me no word? . . . He did not have to do this, Henry. He didn't need to tell you I am a nigger to stop me. . . .

—You are my brother.

—No I'm not. I'm the nigger that's going to sleep with your sister. Unless you stop me, Henry.

Equally, if not more, fascinating is Ernest Hemingway's employment of color-ism. His use of this wholly available device moves through several modes of color-ism—from despicable blacks, to sad but sympathetic ones, to extreme black-fueled eroticism. None of these categories is outside the writer's world or his or her imaginative prowess, but how that world is articulated is what interests me. Color-ism is so very available—it is the ultimate narrative shortcut.

Note Hemingway's employment of color-ism in *To Have and Have Not* (*The Tradesman's Return*). When Harry Morgan, a rum smuggler and the novel's main character, speaks directly to the only black character in the boat, he calls him by his name, Wesley. But when Hemingway's narrator addresses the reader he says (writes) "nigger." Here the two men, who are in Morgan's boat, have both been shot up after a run-in with Cuban officials:

> . . . and he said to the nigger, "Where the hell are we?"
>
> The nigger raised himself up to look. . . .
>
> "I'm going to make you comfortable, Wesley," he said. . . .
>
> "I can't even move," the nigger said. . . .
>
> He gave the Negro a cup of water. . . .
>
> The nigger tried to move to reach a sack, then groaned and lay back.

"Do you hurt that bad, Wesley?"

"Oh, God," the nigger said.

Why the actual name of his companion isn't enough to drive, explain, or describe their venture is not clear—unless the author intends to pinpoint the narrator's compassion for a black man, a compassion that might endear this bootlegger to readers.

Now compare that rendering of a black man as constantly complaining, weak, and in need of his (more seriously injured) white boss's help with another of Hemingway's manipulations of racial tropes—this time for erotic, highly desirable effect.

In *The Garden of Eden,* the male character, called "the young man" first and David later, is on an extended honeymoon on the Côte d'Azur with his new bride, called alternately "the girl" and Catherine. They lounge, swim, eat, and make love over and over. Their conversation is mostly inconsequential chatter or confessions, but running through it is a dominating theme of physical blackness as profoundly beautiful, exciting, and sexually compelling:

". . . you're my good lovely husband and my brother too. . . . when we go to Africa I'll be your African girl too."

[. . . .]

"It's too early to go to Africa now. It's the big rains and afterwards the grass is too high and it's very cold."

[. . . .]

"Then where should we go?"

"We can go to Spain but . . . It's too early for the Basque coast. It's still cold and rainy. It rains everywhere there now."

"Isn't there a hot part where we could swim the way we do here?"

"You can't swim in Spain the way we do here. You'd get arrested."

"What a bore. Let's wait to go there then because I want us to get darker."

"Why do you want to be so dark?"

". . . Doesn't it make you excited to have
me getting so dark"?
"Uh-huh. I love it."

This strange brew of incest, black skin, and sex-
uality is so unlike Hemingway's separation of
"Cubans" from "niggers" in *To Have and Have
Not*. Although in that novel both in fact refer
to Cubans (people born in Cuba), the latter is
deprived of nationality and a home.

There is a perfectly good reason for the part
color-ism plays in literature. It was the law. Even
a casual examination of the "so-called" color
laws makes the case for the emphasis on color
as indicator of what is legal and what is not. The
legislative acts of Virginia to enforce slavery and
to control blacks (collected by June Purcell
Guild as *Black Laws of Virginia*) are, as the foreword notes, representative of laws which "perme-
ated the life of the eighteenth and nineteenth
century Negro, whether slave or free; and by
implication, the fabric of life for the white
majority."

For example, a statute of 1705 stated that "Popish recusants, convicts, Negroes, mulattoes, and Indian servants, and others not being Christians, shall be incapable to be witnesses in any cases whatsoever."

According to a criminal code of 1847, "Any white person assembling with slaves or free Negroes for purpose of instructing them to read or write . . . shall be confined in jail not exceeding six months and fined not exceeding $100.00."

Much later, under Jim Crow, the *General Code of the City of Birmingham of 1944* prohibited any negro and white, in any public space, from playing together in "any game with cards, dice, dominoes or checkers."

Those laws are archaic and, in a way, silly. And while they are no longer enforced or enforceable, they have laid the carpet on which many writers have danced to great effect.

THE cultural mechanics of becoming American are clearly understood. A citizen of Italy or

Russia immigrates to the United States. She keeps much or some of the language and customs of her home country. But if she wishes to be American—to be known as such and to actually belong—she must become a thing unimaginable in her home country: she must become white. It may be comfortable for her or uncomfortable, but it lasts and has advantages as well as certain freedoms.

Africans and their descendants never had that choice, as so much literature illustrates. I became interested in the portrayal of blacks by culture rather than skin color: when color alone was their bête noire, when it was incidental, and when it was unknowable, or deliberately withheld. The latter offered me an interesting opportunity to ignore the fetish of color as well as a certain freedom accompanied by some very careful writing. In some novels I theatricalized the point by not only refusing to rest on racial signs but also alerting the reader to my strategy.

In *Paradise* the opening sentences launch the ploy: "They shoot the white girl first. With the rest they can take their time." This is meant to be an explosion of racial identification which is subsequently withheld throughout descriptions of the community of women in the convent where the attack takes place. Does the reader search for her, the white girl? Or does he or she lose interest in the search? Abandoning it to concentrate on the substance of the novel? Some readers have told me of their guess, but only one of them was ever correct. Her focus was on behavior—something she identified as a gesture or assumption no black girl would make or have—no matter where she came from or whatever her past. This raceless community neighbors one with exactly the opposite priority—race purity is everything to its members. Anyone who isn't "eight rock," the deepest level of a coal mine, is excluded from their town.

In other works, such as *The Bluest Eye,* the consequences of the color fetish are the theme: its severely destructive force.

I tried again in *Home* to create a work in which color was erased but could be easily assumed if the reader paid close attention to the codes, the restrictions black people routinely suffered: where one sits on a bus, where one urinates, and so on. But I was so very successful in forcing the reader to ignore color that it made my editor nervous. So, reluctantly, I layered in references that verified Frank Money, the main character's, race. I believe it was a mistake that defied my purpose.

In *God Help the Child,* color is both a curse and a blessing, a hammer and a golden ring. Although neither, the hammer nor the ring, helped make the character a sympathetic human being. Only caring unselfishly for somebody else would accomplish true maturity.

There are so many opportunities to reveal race in literature—whether one is conscious of it or not. But writing non-colorist literature about black people is a task I have found both liberating and hard.

How much tension or interest would Ernest Hemingway have lost if he had simply used

Wesley's given name? How much fascination and shock would be dampened if Faulkner had limited the book's central concern to incest rather than the theatrical "one-drop" curse?

Some readers coming for the first time to *A Mercy*, which takes place two years before the Salem witch trials, may assume that only blacks were slaves. But so too might be a Native American, or a white homosexual couple, like the characters in my novel. The white mistress in *A Mercy*, though not enslaved, was purchased in an arranged marriage.

I first tried this technique of racial erasure in a short story titled "Recitatif." It began as a screenplay that I was asked to write for two actresses—one black, one white. But since in the writing I didn't know which actress would play which part, I eliminated color altogether, using social class as the marker. The actresses didn't like my play at all. Later I converted the material into a short story—which, by the way, does exactly the opposite of my plan (the characters are divided by race, but all racial codes have been deliberately removed). Instead of relating to plot and character development, most readers insist on searching for what I have refused them.

My effort may not be admired by or interesting to other black authors. After decades of struggle to write powerful narratives portraying decidedly black characters, they may wonder if I am engaged in literary white-washing. I am not. And I am not asking to be joined in this endeavor. But I am determined to de-fang cheap racism, annihilate and discredit the routine, easy, available color fetish, which is reminiscent of slavery itself.

4

Configurations of Blackness

THE DEFINITIONS of "black" and descriptions of what blackness means are so varied and loaded with slippery science and invention that it may be interesting, if not definitively clarifying, to examine the terms' configurations and the literary uses to which they are put as well as the activity they inspire—both violent and constructive.

I have delved somewhat closely into the history of Oklahoma's black towns. Land appropriated (under duress) from the Comanche tribes, known as Oklahoma Territory and Indian Territory, was declared "free" to homesteaders.

Among those who staked claims on this newly available land were freedmen and former slaves who founded some fifty towns. Out of that fifty, I understand, some thirteen still exist: Langston (where Langston University was built), Boley (which supported two colleges—Creek-Seminole College and Methodist Episcopal College), Tullahassee, Red Bird, Vernon, Tatums, Brooksville, Grayson, Lima, Summit, Renstiesville, Taft, and Clearview.

Not all of the inhabitants were black-skinned; a very few were Native Americans and Europeans. But they defined themselves and accepted government help as black people. What the founders of these towns meant by "black" is not always clear. After the Civil War, as ex-slaves migrated to the North and the Midwest, many, many advertisements and solicitations cautioned: "Come prepared, or not at all." That seemed to be sage advice: bring your own tools, horses, clothing, money, and skills so you will not be a burden and can make your own way. Yet it was exclusionary—an elderly widow with no skills but housekeeping? a mother with small children and no husband? a physically disabled old man? Such people would have been warned away to ensure the health and growth of the town. Also, it seemed to me, mixed-race pioneers were preferable. I gathered that from looking at photographs showing the one or two dark-skinned men assigned to guard duty. Thriving black towns were apparently peopled by the light-skinned—meaning they had "white" blood in their veins.

I make a point of this color distinction for two reasons. One is that the meaning of color and its so-called characteristics have been the subject of scholarly and political discussion for at least a century. Another is the effect that the "meaning" has had on the so-called black and white population. (It should be mentioned that Africans—except for South Africans—do not call themselves "black." They are Ghanaians, Nigerians, Kenyans, etc.)

Huge amounts of medical and scientific scholarship have been devoted to the question (assuming it is a question) of what kind of species black people are and what characteristics they possess. The language invented by these investigators in the nineteenth century for various "disorders," as we have seen, is astounding: "dyaesthesia aethiopica" (rascality in blacks free and enslaved), "drapetomania" (a tendency among the enslaved to flee captivity). These terms surely have contributed to racism and its spread, which even now we take for granted. (What would we be or do or become as a society if there were no ranking or theory of blackness?)

Once blackness is accepted as socially, politically, and medically defined, how does that definition affect black people?

We have noted the growth of black towns, harbors of safety and prosperity as far away as possible from white people. What must life have been like for the black inhabitants, living in a world surrounded by hostility and threats of death? Indeed, just how safe were they, considering what they knew of the world around them? Earlier I said that of the fifty or so black towns founded in Oklahoma between 1865 and 1920 some thirteen remain in existence. Of the thirty-seven or so that do not, their inhabitants may have witnessed firsthand the reason they escaped in the first place and wondered anew what black life was worth. Certainly if they were around in 1946.

The United States in the twentieth century had not moved away from eugenics, nor had there been a significant lull in lynchings. Photographs of dead black bodies surrounded by happy white onlookers appeared in print, and postcards of lynchings were a popular item.

The fear that black people had was not fantasy or a pathological condition.

It was in 1946 that Isaac Woodard, a black veteran still in uniform, stepped off a Greyhound bus in South Carolina. He was returning to

North Carolina to join his family. He had spent four years in the army—in the Pacific Theater (where he was promoted to sergeant) and in the Asiatic Pacific (where he earned a Campaign medal, a World War II Victory Medal, and the Good Conduct Medal). When the bus reached a rest stop, he asked the bus driver if there was time to use the restroom. They argued, but he was allowed to use the facilities. Later, when the bus stopped in Batesburg, South Carolina, the driver called the police to remove Sergeant Woodard (apparently for going to the bathroom). The chief, Linwood Shull, took Woodard to a nearby alleyway where he and a number of other policemen beat him with their nightsticks. Then they took him to jail and arrested him for disorderly conduct. During his night in jail, the chief of police beat Woodard with a billy club and gouged out his eyes. The next morning Woodard was sent before the local judge, who found him guilty and fined him fifty dollars. Woodard asked for medical care and two days later it arrived. Meantime, not knowing where he was and suffering from mild amnesia, he was taken to a hospital in Aiken, South Carolina. Three weeks after he was reported missing by his family, he was located and rushed to an army hospital in Spartanburg. Both eyes remained damaged beyond repair. He lived, though blind, until 1992, when he died at age seventy-three. After thirty minutes of deliberation, Chief Shull was acquitted of all charges, to the wild applause of an all-white jury.

Why that attack—in addition to the coverage it received from the NAACP and other organizations—got the attention of President Harry Truman while so many others did not can be attributed to the medals the victim had on his uniform displaying his battlefield deployments and commendations.

What might these black towns fear? Isaac Woodard was not alone.

Let me mention just a small handful of the lynchings that took place in the twentieth century:

Ed Johnson, 1906 (lynched on the Walnut Street Bridge, in Chattanooga, Tennessee, by a mob that broke into jail after a stay of execution had been issued).

Laura and L. D. Nelson, 1911 (mother and son, accused of murder, kidnapped from their cell, hanged from a railroad bridge near Okemah, Oklahoma).

Elias Clayton, Elmer Jackson, and Isaac McGhie, 1920 (three circus workers accused of rape without any evidence, lynched in Duluth, Minnesota; no punishment for their murderers).

Raymond Gunn, 1931 (accused of rape and murder, doused with gasoline and burned to death by a mob in Maryville, Missouri).

Cordie Cheek, 1933 (lynched and mutilated by a mob in Maury, Tennessee, following his release from jail after being falsely accused of rape).

Booker Spicely, 1944 (shot by a bus driver in Durham, North Carolina, after refusing to move further to the back of the bus).

Maceo Snipes, 1946 (dragged from his home in Taylor County, Georgia, and shot for having voted in the Georgia Democratic Primary; a sign posted on a nearby black church read: THE FIRST NIGGER TO VOTE WILL NEVER VOTE AGAIN).

Lamar Smith, 1955 (civil rights figure, shot to death on the lawn of the Lincoln County Courthouse in Brookhaven, Mississippi).

Emmett Till, 1955 (at fourteen years of age, beaten and shot in Money, Mississippi, after reportedly flirting with a white woman who has since confessed to lying about the encounter).

These are just some—there are many, many more, all dreadful—but these are representative, I think, of the circumstances, the real danger for blacks (no longer slaves) in the twentieth century.

So they fled to "free" land and established their own hierarchy of color, ranking the deepest black—"blue black"—skin as a definitive mark of acceptability. This is, anyway, the premise of my novel *Paradise,* concerning the remote (fictional) all-black town of Ruby, Oklahoma, where there is "nothing to serve a traveler: no diner, no police, no gas station, no public phone, no movie house, no hospital."

Color coding among blacks themselves, the threat of being turned away by members of one's own race, as well as the severe possibility of being brutalized in the same way and for the same non-reason Isaac Woodard was, were the realities that motivated the founders of many black towns. In *Paradise,* I imagined a reverse dystopia—a deepening of the definition of "black" and a search for its purity as defiance against the eugenics of "white" purity and especially the "Come Prepared or Not at All" rule which would exclude many, many poor blacks escaping with nothing on their backs.

What might be the reason for and success of an all-black town that emphasized its own standards of purity? In *Paradise* I wanted to reconfigure blackness.

I wanted to trace the purity requirement and the response by the townspeople when black purity was threatened by the lesser or the impure.

In *Paradise,* I played with these confused and confusing concepts of blackness. I began at the very opening, which signals race, purity, and violence: "They shoot the white girl first. With the rest they can take their time." Just as the "white girl" is never identified, none of the killers is given a name in the initial onslaught. The men committing the murders are a son or nephew or brother, uncle, friend, brother-in-law—but no proper names.

After this deliberate anonymity, each of the following chapters is headed by a woman's name: Mavis, Grace, Seneca, Divine, Patricia, Consolata, Lone, and Save-Marie, without identifying her "race."

I was eager to simultaneously de-fang and theatricalize race, signaling, I hoped, how moveable and hopelessly meaningless the construct was. What more, really, do you know about these characters when you do know their race? Anything?

The threats in the world "outside" Ruby, the townsmen's familiarity with the danger they face by being black, define their determination to build a racially pure black town they can control and defend:

Ten generations had known what lay Out There: space, once beckoning and free, became unmonitored and seething; became a void where random and organized evil erupted when and where it chose—behind any standing tree, behind the door of any house, humble or grand. Out There where your children were sport, your women quarry, and where your very person could be annulled; where congregations carried arms to church and ropes coiled in every saddle. Out There where every cluster of whitemen looked like a posse, being alone was being dead. But lessons had been learned and relearned in the last three generations about how to protect a town. So, like the ex-slaves who knew what came first . . . Before first light in the middle of August, fifteen families moved . . . headed not for Muskogee or California as some had, or Saint Louis, Houston, Langston or Chicago, but deeper into Oklahoma. . . .

The Morgan Brothers control the town they helped found, which they name Ruby to honor their recently dead sister. Despite their local power and threats, however, deep and severe conflicts exist among the townspeople. One of the most disrupting is the question of what the engraving (missing the first letter) on their precious community Oven, built by the Old Fathers and transported to Ruby, says. Is it "Be

The Furrow of His Brow"? Or, as the young people insist, "We Are The Furrow of His Brow"? Or even "Women Are the Furrow of His Brow"? And along with frowned-upon sexual liaisons with outsiders, there is a fundamental religious division. The sermons of Reverend Pulliam, an arrogant conservative preacher, illustrate one of the town's divisions. His sermon at a wedding is a sample:

> Let me tell you about love, that silly word you believe is about whether you like some-body or whether somebody likes you or whether you can put up with somebody in order to get something or some place you want or you believe it has to do with how your body responds to another body like robins or bison or maybe you believe love is how forces or nature or luck is benign to you in particular not maiming or killing you but if so doing it for your own good.

Love is none of that. There is nothing in nature like it. Not in robins or bison or the banging tails of your hunting dogs and not in blossoms or suckling foal. Love is divine only and difficult always. If you think it is easy you are a fool. If you think it is natural you are blind. It is a learned application without reason or motive except that it is God.

You do not deserve love regardless of the suffering you have endured. You do not deserve love because somebody did you wrong. You do not deserve love just because you want it. You can only earn—by practice and careful contemplation—the right to express it and you have to learn how to accept it. Which is to say you have to earn God. You have to practice God. You have to think God—carefully. And if you are a good and diligent student you may secure the right to show love. Love is not a gift. It is a diploma. A diploma conferring certain privileges: the privilege of expressing love and the privilege of receiving it.

How do you know you have graduated? You don't. What you do know is that you are human and therefore educable, and therefore capable of learning how to learn, and therefore interesting to God, who is interested only in Himself which is to say He is interested only in love. Do you understand me? God is not interested in you. He is interested in love and the bliss it brings to those who understand and share that interest.

The counter to that view of God is articulated by Reverend Misner, the progressive preacher presiding over the wedding, for whom love is "unmotivated respect: All of which testified not to a peevish Lord who was His own love but one who enabled human love. Not for His own glory—never. God loved the way humans loved

one another; loved the way humans loved themselves; loved the genius on the cross who man-
aged to do both and die knowing it." In silent
protest against Pulliam's "poison," he holds up
a cross before the congregation, thinking,

See? The execution of this one solitary black
man propped up on these two intersecting
lines to which he was attached in a parody
of human embrace, fastened to two big
sticks that were so convenient, so recogniz-
able, so embedded in consciousness *as
consciousness,* being both ordinary and sub-
lime. See? His woolly head alternately rising
on his neck and falling toward his chest,
the glow of his midnight skin dimmed by
dust, streaked by gall, fouled by spit and
urine, gone pewter in the hot, dry wind
and, finally, as the sun dimmed in shame,
as his flesh matched the odd lessening of
afternoon light as though it were evening,
always sudden in that climate, swallowing

him and the other death row felons, and the silhouette of this original sign merged with a false night sky. See how this official murder out of hundreds marked the difference; moved the relationship between God and man from CEO and supplicant to one on one? The cross he held was abstract; the absent body was real, but both combined to pull humans from backstage to the spotlight, from muttering in the wings to the principal role in the story of their lives. This execution made it possible to respect— freely, not in fear—one's self and one another.

The conflicts within Ruby grow, so much so that the men (some of them) need desperately to find an enemy to purge and destroy the evil and disruption in their community. The women in a nearby former convent, outside of Ruby, serve that purpose beautifully.

Of course the women—a collection of misfits and fugitives—are no peaceful saints. They disagree about virtually everything except their affection for the convent's last inhabitant, an old drunken woman named Consolata who welcomes them all. Prior to the violence that the men of Ruby inflict on the women, Consolata demands an extraordinary ritual called "loud dreaming," one that cleanses and empowers each woman in the convent. Too late. The men of Ruby descend.

Amid all of this struggle, chaos, and unbreakable conflict caused by power distribution within classifications of race and gender, I hoped to draw attention to specific individuals trying to escape harm and mitigate their failures—one narrative at a time. One to one.

The work—or my purpose in writing it— reminds me of something I experienced years ago at a Vienna Biennale. In one of the artworks on display, I was asked to enter a dark room and face a mirror. In a few seconds a figure appeared, slowly taking shape and moving toward me. A woman. When she (rather, her image) was close to me, same height, she placed her palm on the glass and I was instructed to do the same. We stood there face to face, unspeaking, looking into the eyes of the other. Slowly the figure faded and shrank before disappearing altogether. Another woman appeared. We repeated the gesture of touching our palms together and looking into the eyes of the other. This went on for some time. Each woman differed in age, body shape, color, dress. I must say it was extraordinary—this intimacy with a stranger. Silent, knowing. Accepting each other—one to one.

5

Narrating the Other

I SPENT many years as a senior editor at Random House—about nineteen years—determined to include as many excellent African American writers as possible in the publisher's catalogue.

Several of the projects I brought to my editorial committee were approved: books by Toni Cade Bambara, Angela Davis, Gayl Jones, and Huey Newton, among others. Other than Muhammad Ali's autobiography, the sales were unimpressive. The subject came up at a sales conference one day when a regional salesman said it was not possible to sell books "on both sides of the street." He meant that white people bought most books, blacks fewer, if any at all.

I thought to myself, well, what if I published a book good enough, attractive enough to demand black people's attention? So I began to imagine what became *The Black Book,* an elegant scrapbook of photographs, lyrics, patents of inventions by black people, news clippings, advertising posters—everything about African American history and culture, the awful and horrendous as well as the beautiful and triumphant. The material came from everywhere, but especially from collectors who had boxes and files of American and African American history.

Among the material I collected was a newspaper clipping with the intriguing headline "A Visit to the Slave Mother Who Killed Her Child." It was published in the February 12, 1856, issue of the *American Baptist,* by Reverend P. S. Bassett, from the Fairmount Theological

Seminary in Cincinnati, Ohio, who made it his duty to worship with prisoners. Margaret Garner, the slave mother, and members of her family had fled Kentucky, where they were enslaved, for the free state of Ohio. Bassett's encounter with Margaret Garner reads:

Last Sabbath, after preaching in the city prison, Cincinnati, through the kindness of the Deputy Sheriff, I was permitted to visit the apartment of that unfortunate woman, concerning whom there has been so much excitement during the last two weeks.

I found her with an infant in her arms only a few months old, and observed that it had a large [bruise] on its forehead. I inquired the cause of the injury. She then proceeded to give a detailed account of her attempt to kill her children.

She said, that when the officers and slave-hunters came to the house in which they were concealed, she caught a shovel and struck two of her children on the head, and then took a knife and cut the throat of the third, and tried to kill the other—that if they had given her time, she would have killed them all—that with regard to herself, she cared but little; but she was unwilling to have her children suffer as she had done.

I inquired if she was not excited almost to madness when she committed the act. No, she replied, I was as cool as I now am; and would much rather kill them at once and thus end their sufferings than have them taken back to slavery and be murdered by piece-meal. She then told the story of her wrongs. She spoke of her days of suffering, of her nights of unmitigated toil, while the bitter tears coursed their way down her cheeks, and fell in the face of the innocent child as it looked smiling up, little conscious of the danger and probable sufferings that awaited it.

As I listened to the facts and witnessed the agony depicted in her countenance, I could not but exclaim, O, how terrible is irresponsible power when exercised over intelligent beings! She alludes to the child that she killed as being free from all trouble and sorrow with a degree of satisfaction that almost chills the blood in one's veins. Yet she evidently possesses all the passionate tenderness of a mother's love. She is about twenty-five years of age, and apparently possesses an average amount of kindness, with a vigorous intellect, and much energy of character.

The two men and the two other children were in another apartment, but her mother-in-law was in the same room. [The mother-in-law] says she is the mother of eight children, most of whom have been separated from her; that her husband was once separated from her twenty-five years, during which time she did not see him; that could she have prevented it, she

would never have permitted him to return, as she did not wish him to witness
her sufferings, or be exposed to the brutal
treatment that he would receive.

She states that she has been a faithful
servant; and in her old age she would not
have attempted to obtain her liberty; but as
she became feeble and less capable of per-
forming labor, her master became more
and more exacting and brutal in his treatment, until she could stand it no longer;
that the effort could only result in death, at
most—she therefore made the attempt.

She witnessed the killing of the child,
but said she neither encouraged nor dis-
couraged her daughter-in-law—for under
similar circumstances she would probably
have done the same. The old woman is
from sixty to seventy years of age, has
been a professor of religion about twenty
years, and speaks with much feeling of
the time when she shall be delivered from

the power of the oppressor, and dwell with the Savior, "where the wicked cease from troubling, and the weary are at rest."

These slaves (as far as I am informed) have resided all their lives within sixteen miles of Cincinnati. We are frequently told that Kentucky slavery is very innocent. If these are its fruits, where it exists in a mild form, will some one tell us what we may expect from its more objectionable features? But comments are unnecessary.

The observations in that article that called my attention were: 1) the mother-in-law's inability to condemn or approve the infanticide; and 2) Margaret Garner's serenity.

As some of my readers know, Margaret Garner's story was the genesis for my novel *Beloved* (1987). Some ten years after the publication of the novel, a biography of the historical Margaret Garner was published. Its title is *Modern Medea: A Family Story of Slavery and*

Child-Murder from the Old South, by Steven Weisenburger. While the reference in Mr. Weisenburger's book is to the classical story of a spurned woman who killed her children as an act of vengeance against their unfaithful father, my narrative is about the understandable versus the savage act of child murder.

Weisenburger's biography is a thorough examination of the facts surrounding Margaret Garner's actions and their consequences—facts I knew little to nothing of and which I deliberately chose not to investigate even if I had had the opportunity, which I didn't. I wanted to rely fully on my own imagination. My principal interest was in trying to fathom the mother-in-law's inability to condemn her daughter-in-law for murder.

Wondering what her answer might finally be, I decided that the only one with the unquestionable right to judge was the dead child herself, whom I named the one word her mother could have afforded to have inscribed on her tombstone, Beloved. Of course I changed names, created characters, eliminated characters, and shrunk others (for example, Margaret Garner's husband, Robert), and I ignored the trial completely (which was months long, controversial, and roiled abolitionists, who turned Garner into a *cause célèbre* as they tried to get her charged with murder in an effort to overturn the Fugitive Slave Law of 1850). And in any case, had I known, I would have ignored the fact that several of her children were mixed-race, a clear sign that her owner raped her—easily, since her husband was frequently sent away to work at other plantations. I gave her one surviving child, the birth of whom was aided by a white girl, a runaway slave herself, whose sympathy was based on gender, not race. I saw Sethe, the name I gave the mother, escaping alone. I inserted a speaking, thinking dead child whose impact—and appearance and disappearance—could operate as slavery's gothic damage. And I gave the mother-in-law (Baby Suggs) a pivotal role in enduring slavery as an un-churched, self-chosen preacher. And I hoped to explain her reluctance to condemn her daughter-in-law by her faith and commitment to love in her sermon.

This is part of it, the sermon Baby Suggs delivers in the clearing in the woods:

"Here," she said, "in this here place, we flesh; flesh that weeps, laughs; flesh that dances on bare feet in grass. Love it. Love it hard. Yonder they do not love your flesh. They despise it. They don't love your eyes; they'd just as soon pick em out. No more do they love the skin on your back. Yonder they flay it. And O my people they do not love your hands. Those they only use, tie, bind, chop off and leave empty. Love your hands! Love them. Raise them up and kiss them. Touch others with them, pat them together, stroke them on your face 'cause they don't love that either. *You* got to love it, *you!* And no, they ain't in love with your mouth. Yonder, out there, they will see it broken and break it again. What you say out of it they will not heed. What you scream from it they do not hear. What you put into it to nourish your body they will snatch away and give you leavins instead. No they don't love your mouth. *You* got to love it . . . And O my people, out yonder, hear me they do not love your neck un-noosed and straight. So love your neck; put a hand on it, grace it, stroke it and hold it up. And all your inside parts that they'd just as soon slop for hogs you got to love them. The dark, dark liver— love it, love it, and the beat and beating heart, love that too. More than eyes or feet. More than lungs that have yet to draw free air. More than your life-holding womb and your life-giving private parts, hear me now, love your heart. For this is the prize."

I enhanced the life of the saved child, named her Denver, after the white girl who had helped her mother deliver her, and explored what her life was like living with a mother who had killed her sister, but who had the emotional and literal help of her grandmother and neighbors—enough to embolden her and make it possible for her to thrive.

I created my own version of the end, which I chose to make hopeful, unlike the sad, disturbing, and true end of Margaret Garner's life. Re-named and re-drawn as Sethe, my slave mother is encouraged finally to think, even know, that she may be a valuable human in spite of what happened to her and her daughter. "She was my best thing," she tells Paul D, referring to Beloved. He says, no, "You are your best thing." She questions it: "Me? Me?" She is not certain, but at least the idea interests her. So there is the possibility of union, of peace, of having no need for regret.

That ending, of course, was not the final word. That would have to belong to the Other, the prime motivator, the reason for the novel's existence, Beloved herself:

There is a loneliness that can be rocked. Arms crossed, knees drawn up; holding, holding on, this motion, unlike a ship's, smooths and contains the rocker. It's an inside kind—wrapped tight like skin. Then there is a loneliness that roams. No rocking can hold it down. It is alive, on its own. A dry and spreading thing that makes the sound of one's own feet going seem to come from a far-off place.

Everybody knew what she was called, but nobody anywhere knew her name. Disremembered and unaccounted for, she cannot be lost because no one is looking for her, and even if they were, how can they call her if they don't know her name? Although she has claim, she is not claimed. In the place where long grass opens, the girl who waited to be loved and cry shame erupts into her separate parts, to make it easy for the chewing laughter to swallow her all away.

It was not a story to pass on.

They forgot her like a bad dream. After they made up their tales, shaped and decorated them, those that saw her that day on the porch quickly and deliberately forgot her. It took longer for those who had spoken to her, lived with her, fallen in love with her, to forget, until they realized they couldn't remember or repeat a single thing she said, and began to believe that, other than what they themselves were thinking, she hadn't said anything at all. So, in the end, they forgot her too. Remembering seemed unwise. They never knew where or why she crouched, or whose was the underwater face she needed like that. Where the memory of the smile under her chin might have been and was not, a latch latched and lichen attached its apple-green bloom to the metal. What made her think her fingernails could open locks the rain rained on?

It was not a story to pass on.

So they forgot her. Like an unpleasant dream during a troubling sleep. Occasionally, however, the rustle of a skirt hushes when they wake, and the knuckles brushing a cheek in sleep seem to belong to the sleeper. Sometimes the photograph of a close friend or relative— looked at too long—shifts, and something more familiar than the dear face itself moves there. They can touch it if they like, but don't, because they know things will never be the same if they do.

This is not a story to pass on.

Down by the stream in back of 124 her footprints come and go, come and go. They are so familiar. Should a child, an adult place his feet in them, they will fit. Take them out and they disappear again as though nobody ever walked there.

By and by all trace is gone, and what is forgotten is not only the footprints but the water too and what it is down there. The rest is weather. Not the breath of the disremembered and unaccounted for, but wind in the eaves, or spring ice thawing too quickly. Just weather. Certainly no clamor for a kiss.

Beloved.

The outcome of the actual trial I knew: the slave mother was in effect judged to have no legal responsibility for the killing of her child (if found responsible, she would have been condemned to death), as a Federal District Court judge stepped in to rule that the Fugitive Slave Act must take precedence. Margaret Garner was therefore under the law a piece of property, as were her offspring—who in no way belonged to her—because they were stock that could be—and regularly were—sold. Which is to say Garner was finally judged not human with human responsibilities, such as motherhood, but as an animal to be sold like cattle. In any case, she was doomed: to early death as a killer or slow death as a brutalized slave. In fact, as Mr. Weisenburger discovered, she was sent South again and lived as a slave until she died of typhoid in 1858.

Compelling as the real Margaret Garner's story is, the novel's center and spread are the murdered child. Imagining her was for me the soul of art and its bones.

Narrative fiction provides a controlled wilderness, an opportunity to be and to become the Other. The stranger. With sympathy, clarity, and the risk of self-examination. In this iteration, for me the author, Beloved the girl, the haunter, is the ultimate Other. Clamoring, forever clamoring for a kiss.

6

The Foreigner's Home

Excluding the height of the slave trade in the nineteenth century, the mass movement of peoples in the latter half of the twentieth century and the beginning of the twenty-first is greater than it has ever been. It is a movement of workers, intellectuals, refugees, and immigrants, crossing oceans and continents, through customs offices or in flimsy boats, speaking multiple languages of trade, of political intervention, of persecution, war, violence, and poverty. There is little doubt that the re-distribution (voluntary and involuntary) of people all over the globe tops the agenda of the state, the boardrooms, the neighborhoods, the street. Political maneuvers to control this movement are not limited to monitoring the dispossessed and / or holding them hostage. Much of this exodus can be described as the journey of the colonized to the seat of the colonizers (slaves, as it were, leaving the plantation for the planters' home), while more of it is the flight of war refugees, and (less of it) the relocation and transplantation of the management and diplomatic class to globalization's outposts. The establishment of military bases and the deployment of fresh military units feature prominently in legislative attempts to control the constant flow of people.

The spectacle of mass movement draws attention inevitably to the borders, the porous places, the vulnerable points where the concept of home is seen as being menaced by foreigners. Much of the alarm hovering at the borders, the gates, is stoked, it seems to me, by 1) both the threat and the promise of globalization; and 2) an uneasy relationship with our own foreignness, our own rapidly disintegrating sense of belonging.

Let me begin with globalization. In our current understanding, globalization is not a version of the nineteenth-century "Britannia Rules" format—although post-colonial upheavals reflect and are reminiscent of the domination one nation (Great Britain) then had over most others. The term "globalization" does not have the "workers of the world unite" agenda of the old proletarian internationalism—although that was the very word, "internationalism," that the now former president of the AFL-CIO, John Sweeney, used at the Executive Council of Union Presidents when he spoke of the need for American unions to "build a new internationalism." Nor is this globalization the same as the post-war appetite for "one world," the rhetoric that stirred and bedeviled the 1950s and launched the United Nations. Nor is it the "universalism" of the 1960s and 1970s—either as a plea for world peace or as an insistence on cultural hegemony. "Empire," "internationalism," "one world," "universal"—all seem less like categories of historical trends and more like yearnings. Yearnings to corral the earth into some semblance of unity and some measure of control, or to conceive of the planet's human destiny as flowing from one constellation of nations' ideology. Globalization has the same desires and yearnings as its predecessors. It too understands itself as historically progressive, enhancing, unifying, utopian, and destined. Narrowly defined, it means the free movement of capital and the rapid distribution of data and products operating within a politically neutral environment shaped by multinational corporate demands. Its larger connotations, however, are less innocent, encompassing as they do, not only the demonization of embargoed states or the trivialization-cum-negotiation with war lords and corrupt politicians, but also the collapse of nation states under the weight of transnational economics, capital, and labor; the preeminence of Western culture and economy; and the Americanization of the developed and developing world through the penetration of U.S. cultures into the West in fashion, film, music, and cuisine.

Globalization, hailed with the same vigor as was manifest destiny, internationalism, etc., has reached a level of majesty in our imagination. For all its claims of fostering freedom and equality, globalization's dispensations are royal. For it can bestow much, and withhold much, in matters of reach (across frontiers); in terms of mass (the sheer number of people affected positively or negatively); in terms of speed (the emergence of new technologies); and in terms of riches (the exploitation of resources limited only by a finite planet and countless goods and services to be exported and imported). Yet, as much as globalism is adored as near messianic, it is also reviled as an evil courting a dangerous dystopia. We fear its disregard of borders, national infrastructures, local bureaucracies, internet censors, tariffs, laws, and languages; its heed-lessness of margins and marginal people; its formidable, engulfing properties accelerating erasure, a flattening out of meaningful differences. Our abhorrence of diversity notwithstanding, we imagine in-distinguishability, the elimination in the near future of all minority languages and cultures. Or we speculate with horror on what could be the irrevocable, enfeebling alteration of major languages and cultures in globalization's sweep.

Of the many reasons and necessities for the mass movement of peoples, war leads them all. It is estimated that when the final numbers of the displaced come out—those running from persecution, conflict, and generalized violence in today's world (including refugees, asylum seekers, and internally displaced persons)—the number will far surpass sixty million. Sixty million. And half of all refugees are children. I don't know the number of the dead.

Even if our worst fears about the future are not made completely manifest, they nevertheless cancel out globalization's assurances of a better life by issuing dire warnings of premature cultural death.

Once again I want to use literature to comment on the bane (the poison) of foreignness. More particularly, I want to look at a novel written in the 1950s by a Ghanaian author as a means of addressing this dilemma: the inside / outside blur that can enshrine frontiers and borders—real, metaphorical, and psychological—as we wrestle with definitions of nation, state, and citizenship as well as the ongoing problems of racism and race relations, and the so-called clash of cultures in our search to belong.

African and African American writers are not alone in coming to terms with these problems, but they do have a long and singular history of confronting them. Of not being at home in their homeland; of being exiled in the place where they belong.

Before I discuss this novel, I want to describe something from my childhood that long preceded my reading of African literature but nonetheless compelled my excursion into what troubles contemporary definitions of the foreign.

Velvet-lined offering plates were passed down the church pews on Sunday. The last one was the smallest and the one most likely to be left empty. Its position and size signaled the dutiful but limited expectations that characterized most everything in the 1930s. The coins, never bills, sprinkled there were mostly from children encouraged to give up pennies and nickels for the charitable work so necessary for the redemption, the saving, of Africa. Although the sound of the name, Africa, was beautiful, it was freighted with the complicated emotions with which it was associated. Unlike starving China, Africa was both ours and theirs, intimately connected to us and profoundly foreign. A huge needy homeland to which we were said to belong but which none of us had seen or cared to see, inhabited by people with whom we maintained a delicate relationship of mutual ignorance and disdain, and with whom we shared a mythology of passive, traumatized Otherness cultivated by textbooks, film, cartoons, and the hostile name-calling children learn to love.

Later, when I began to read fiction set in Africa, I found that, with few exceptions, each successive narrative elaborated on and enhanced the very mythology that accompanied those velvet plates floating between the pews. For Joyce Cary, Elspeth Huxley, H. Rider Haggard, Africa was precisely what the missionary collection implied: a dark continent in desperate need of light. The light of Christianity, of civilization, of development. The light of charity switched on by simple good-heartedness. It was an idea of Africa fraught with the assumptions of a complex intimacy coupled with an acknowledgment of unmediated estrangement. The conundrum of paternalistic-colonial "elders" alienating the local population, the dispossession of native speakers from their home, the exile of indigenous peoples within their home contributed a surreal glow to these narratives, enticing the writers to project a metaphysically void Africa ripe for invention. With one or two exceptions, literary Africa was an inexhaustible playground for tourists and foreigners. In the works of Joseph Conrad, Isak Dinesen, Saul Bellow, and Ernest Hemingway, whether imbued with or struggling against conventional Western views of a benighted Africa, their protagonists found the world's second largest continent to be as empty as that collection plate—a vessel waiting for whatever copper and silver the imagination was pleased to place there. As grist for Western mills, accommodatingly mute, conveniently blank, indisputably foreign, Africa could be made to support a wide variety of literary and / or ideological requirements. It could withdraw as scenery for any exploit, or leap forward and implicate itself in the woes of any foreigner; it could contort itself into frightening, malignant shapes upon which Westerners could contemplate evil, or it could kneel and accept elementary lessons from its betters. For those who made that literal or imaginative voyage, contact with Africa offered thrilling opportunities to experience life in its primitive, formative, inchoate state, the consequence of which was self-enlightenment—a wisdom that confirmed the benefits of European proprietorship free of the responsibility of gathering much actual intelligence about any African culture. Only a little geography, lots of climate, a few customs and anecdotes sufficed as the canvas upon which a portrait of a wiser, or sadder, or fully reconciled self could be painted. In Western novels published through the 1950s, Africa, like Albert Camus' novel, might be called "The Stranger," offering the occasion for knowledge but keeping its unknowableness intact. In Conrad's *Heart of Darkness,* Marlowe speaks of Africa as a once expansive "white patch [on a map] for a boy to dream gloriously over" that has since filled in with "rivers and lakes and names . . . [and] had ceased to be a blank space of delightful mystery. . . . It had become a place of darkness." What little could be known was enigmatic, repugnant, or hopelessly contradictory. Imaginary Africa was a cornucopia of imponderables that, like the monstrous Grendel in *Beowulf,* resisted explanation. Thus, a plethora of incompatible metaphors can be gleaned from the literature. As the original locus of the human race, Africa is ancient, yet, being under colonial control, it is also infantile. A kind of old fetus always waiting to be born but confounding all midwives. In novel after novel, short story after short story, Africa is simultaneously innocent and corrupt, savage and pure, irrational and wise.

In that racially charged literary context, coming upon Camara Laye's *The Radiance of the King* was shocking. Suddenly the clichéd journey into storybook African darkness either to bring light or to find it is re-imagined. The novel not only summons a sophisticated, wholly African imagistic vocabulary from which to launch a discursive negotiation with the West; it also exploits the images of chaos and infantilism that the conqueror imposes on the native population: the social disorder depicted in Joyce Cary's *Mister Johnson;* the obsession with smells in Elspeth Huxley's *The Flame Trees of Thika;* the European fixation on the meaning of nakedness in H. Rider Haggard's novels, or in Joseph Conrad's fiction, or in virtually all Western travel writing. An unclothed or sparsely clothed body could signify only childish innocence or undisciplined eroticism—never the voyeurism of the observer.

Camara Laye's narrative is, briefly, this: Clarence, a European, has come to Africa for reasons he cannot articulate. There he has gambled, lost, and is heavily in debt to his white compatriots. Now he is hiding among the indigenous population in a dirty inn. Already evicted from the colonialists' hotel, and about to be evicted by the African innkeeper, Clarence finds that the solution to his pennilessness is to rely on his whiteness, his European-ness, and be taken, without question or skills, into the service of the king. He is prevented by a solid crowd of villagers from approaching the king, and his mission is greeted with scorn. He meets a pair of mischief-loving teenagers and a cunning beggar who agree to help him. Under their guidance he travels south, where the king is expected to appear next. By way of Clarence's journey, not wholly unlike a pilgrim's progress, Camara Laye is able to trace and parody the parallel sensibilities of Europe and Africa.

The literary tropes of Africa he employs are exact replicas of perceptions of foreignness: 1) Menace; 2) Depravity; and 3) Incomprehensibility. And it is fascinating to observe Camara Laye's adroit handling of those perceptions.

Menace. Clarence, his protagonist, is stupefied with fear. In spite of noting that the "forests [are] devoted to wine industry," that the landscape is "cultivated," that the people living there give him a "cordial welcome," he sees only inaccessibility, "common hostility," a vertigo of tunnels, and paths barred by thorn hedges. The order and clarity of the landscape are at odds with the menacing jungle in his head.

Depravity. It is Clarence who descends into depravity while enacting the full horror of what Westerners imagine as "going native," the "unclean and cloying weakness" that imperils masculinity. Clarence's blatant enjoyment of and feminine submission to continuous cohabitation reflect his own appetites and his own willful ignorance. Over time, as mulatto children crowd the village, Clarence, the only white person in the region, continues to wonder where they came from. He refuses to believe the obvious— that he has been sold as a stud for the harem.

Incomprehensibility. Camara Laye's Africa is not dark; it is suffused with light: the watery green light of the forest; the ruby red tints of the houses and soil; the sky's "unbearable . . . azure brilliance"; even the scales of the fishwomen, which glimmer "like robes of dying moonlight." Understanding the motives, the sensibilities of the Africans—both wicked and benign— requires only a suspension of belief in an unbreachable difference between humans.

Unpacking the hobbled idioms of the foreigner usurping one's home, of de-legitimizing the native, of reversing the claims of belonging, the novel allows us to experience a white man immigrating to Africa, alone, without a job, without authority, without resources or even a family name. But he has one asset that always works, can only work, in third world countries. He is white, he says, and therefore suited in some ineffable way to be advisor to the king, whom he has never seen, in a country he does not know, among people he neither understands nor wishes to. What begins as a quest for a position of authority, for escape from the contempt of his own countrymen, becomes a searing process of re-education. What counts as intelligence among these Africans is not prejudice but nuance and the ability and willingness to see, to surmise. The European's refusal to meditate coherently on any event except the ones that concern his comfort or survival dooms him. When insight finally seeps through, he feels annihilated by it. This fictional investigation into the limited perceptions of a culture allows us to see the de-racing of a Westerner's experience of Africa without European support, protection, or command. It allows us to re-discover or imagine anew what it feels like to be marginal, ignored, superfluous, foreign; to have one's name never uttered; to be stripped of history or representation; to be sold or exploited labor for the benefit of a presiding family, a shrewd entrepreneur, a local regime. In other words, to become a black slave.

It is a disturbing encounter that may help us deal with the destabilizing pressures and forces of the transglobal tread of peoples. Pressures that can make us cling manically to our own cultures, languages, while dismissing others'; make us rank evil according to the fashion of the day; make us legislate, expel, conform, purge, and pledge allegiance to ghosts and fantasy. Most of all, these pressures can make us deny the foreigner in ourselves and make us resist to the death the commonness of humanity.

After many trials, enlightenment slowly surfaces in Camara Laye's European. Clarence gets his wish to meet the king. But by then he and his purpose have altered. Against the advice of the local people, Clarence crawls naked to the throne, when finally he sees the king, who is a mere boy laden with gold. The "terrifying void that is within [him]"—the void that has been protecting him from disclosure—opens to receive the royal gaze. It is this openness, this crumbling of cultural armor maintained out of fear, this act of unprecedented courage that is the beginning of Clarence's salvation. His bliss and his freedom. The boy king takes him in his arms, and wrapped in that embrace, feeling the beat of the king's young heart, Clarence hears him murmur these exquisite words of authentic belonging, words welcoming him to the human race: "Did you not know that I was waiting for you?"

Acknowledgments

I was pleased to be invited to deliver the 2016 Norton Lectures at Harvard University. Thank you to the Norton Committee: Homi Bhabha, Haden Guest, Sylvanie Guyot, Robb Moss, Richard Peña, Eric Rentschler, Diana Sorensen, David Wang, and Nicholas Watson.

Also, my gratitude to those who introduced these lectures is sincere: Homi Bhabha, Davíd Carrasco, Claire Messud, Henry Louis Gates, Jr., Evelynn M. Hammonds, and Diana Sorensen.

I also wish to acknowledge the work of the staff at the Mahindra Humanities Center, and

Acknowledgments

especially John Kulka of Harvard University Press for his careful guidance. Finally, I send thanks to my assistant, René Boatman, for her editorial and research support.